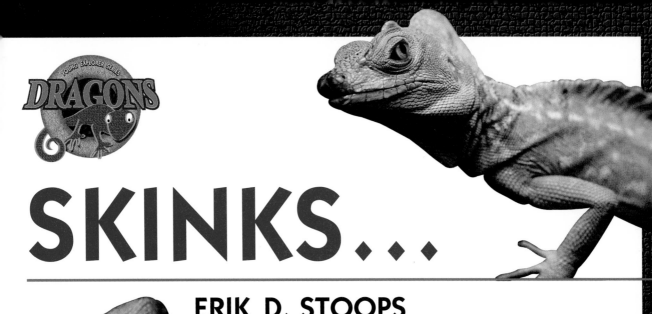

SKINKS...

ERIK D. STOOPS

Faulkner's Publishing Group

This book is dedicated to Sarah Straub for making this book a reality.

Library of Congress Catalog Card Number 97-60518.

COVER PHOTO: African Fire Skink by Terry Odegaard
DESIGNED BY: Graphic Arts & Production Inc., Plover, WI

Faulkner's Publishing Group
200 Paw Paw Ave. #124
Benton Harbor, MI 49022

©1997 by Erik Daniel Stoops
Faulkner's ISBN 1-890475-02-5 Lib

Table of Contents

CHAPTER ONE What is a Skink?..PAGES 4-7

CHAPTER TWO Where are Skinks Found? ....PAGES 8-9

CHAPTER THREE Senses ....PAGES 10-13

CHAPTER FOUR Eating Habits ....PAGES 14-17

CHAPTER FIVE Lizard Reproduction ....PAGES 18-21

CHAPTER SIX Self-Defense..PAGES 22-23

CHAPTER SEVEN Facts about Skinks...PAGES 24-29

Glossary..PAGE 30

Suggested Reading ....PAGE 31

Index ....PAGE 32

Chapter One

What is a Skink?

The lizard is a very interesting reptile.
It has eyelids that blink and odd-looking skin.

What is a Skink?

Are they cold-blooded or warm-blooded?

Read on to find the answers.

5

by Erik D. Stoops

◀ SHINGLEBACK SKINK

What is a Skink?

A Skink is a reptile. These reptiles have four legs for climbing and swimming. They usually have eyelids, ears and a large powerful tail. Some lizards do not have legs at all. Scientists have found that certain lizard species are related to their cousin, the snake.

Are Skinks related to dinosaurs?

According to *herpetologists* and *scientists,* many species of reptiles, including lizards, were thought to be related to the dinosaurs. This is still up for debate. *Paleontologists* have found that the dinosaurs were more closely related to birds.

Are Skinks cold-blooded or warm-blooded?

All species of lizards are *cold-blooded*. They need the warm sun during the day to keep them warm and help them move and digest their food.

AFRICAN FIRE SKINK ▶

by Terry Odegaard

by Erik D. Stoops

▲
SHINGLEBACK SKINK

Shingleback Skink:

This Skink is related to the Blue-Tongued Skink and found only in Australia. They are known as the Pinecone Lizard or Stump-Tailed Skink because the tail looks similar to the head. Most Shingleback Skinks live for a number of years and feed on fruit and insects.

Scientists have found that once the Shingleback Skink finds a mate, it stays with that mate for its entire life. Females give birth to two to four live young.

Spiny-Tailed Skink:

This lizard is found in Australia and is different from other Skinks because of its short, spiny tail. In Australia, it is known as the Gidgee Skink. They feed on small insects and fruit and live in rocky areas where it can hide in crevices and under rocks.

BLUE-TONGUED SKINK
▼

Blue-Tongued Skink:

This lizard is also found throughout Australia and parts of New Guinea. They are known for their bright blue tongues which the lizard uses to smell and eat with. This Skink can reach lengths up to 24 inches.

by Terry Odegaard

Chapter Two

Where are Skinks Found?

Where do Skinks live?

Do Skinks live in water?

Read on to answer these questions and more.

Where do Skinks live?

Lizards can be found all over the world. The greatest number of species reside in the warm zones: deserts, jungles, rain forests, etc. The only place you cannot find a lizard is in the ice-covered polar regions and where temperatures remain ice-cold year-round.

If I want to see a lizard, where should I look?

The safest place to see a lizard is at a zoo. Many zoos have several kinds of species on display from all over the world. It is best not to catch lizards from the wild and keep them in your home. Try to leave them where they belong.

Do Skinks live in water?

No. Some species of Skinks live near water or rely on water for survival. Like any species of lizards, water is very important for daily life.

by Terry Odegaard

▲
MANY SPECIES OF SKINKS MAKE THEIR HOMES IN LARGE TREES LIKE THIS ONE.

Where is the best place to find a Skink?

If I were a Skink, this is where I would be:

- Under a rock
- On a rock
- In a field
- On a house
- In a tree
- In a rain forest

9

Chapter Three

Senses

Lizards have some of the strangest senses of all reptiles.

What would it be like to smell with your tongue
and have eyelids without eyelashes?

Do lizards have ears?

Do lizards shed their skin?

These are some of the questions you will find in this chapter.

11

Do lizards have ears?

Yes. Lizard's ears, which are two tiny holes, are located near their eyes. They can hear vibrations in the air to help them find food and stay safe from their enemies.

◀ THE EARS OF THIS AFRICAN SKINK ARE THE TINY LITTLE HOLES LOCATED BY THE NECK

by Terry Odegaard

SHINGLEBACK SKINK ▶

by Erik D. Stoops

Can lizards see colors?

Scientists have found that certain species of lizards can see colors like red and yellow. Many scientists are still learning about these spectacular findings.

Why do lizards shed their skin?

All species of lizards shed their skin. When a lizard sheds its skin it means that it is growing. Some species of Skinks, such as the Sand Skink, shed in pieces. Other species like the Shingleback Skink, shed in one whole piece.

by Erik D. Stoops

THE SHINGLEBACK SKINK CAN PROBABLY SEE THE VARIOUS COLORED PLANTS AROUND HIM.

How do lizards shed their skin?

When lizards shed their skin, they find something such as a rock or a tree branch to rub on. They try to wiggle out of their skin which usually takes a few hours. After the lizard sheds, it will have bright new, shiny skin.

Do lizards have noses used for smelling?

No. Under their tongue is a mechanism called a Jacobson's organ. This is a smelling organ that helps the lizard find food.

13

Chapter Four

Eating Habits

How often do Skinks eat?

Do lizards chew their food?

Read on to find these answers and more.

Do Skinks get fat?

In captivity, Skink species that do not get very much exercise often become overweight. This is not very healthy for lizards and can cause diseases.

What do Skinks eat?

Skinks eat many different things like mammals, reptiles, insects, fish and snails. Each species has its own type of food it eats. The Prairie Skink likes to eat crickets. The Shingleback Skink likes to eat fruit and will even eat dog food if being held in captivity.

by Bill LuBack's Reptiles

BLUE-TONGUED SKINK

How often do Skinks eat?

Most species will feed almost every day. Smaller species like the Little Brown Skink also gets moisture, "water," from the crickets it eats.

SHINGLEBACK SKINK ▶

16

by Erik D. Stoops

by Terry Odegaard

How do lizards capture their food?

Lizards use their eyesight and strong sense of smell to find food. Insect-eating lizards may stay at a cricket nest and feed until all are full.

Do lizards chew their food?

No. They swallow their food whole. They use their teeth for tearing chunks and then swallow. Some lizards have very small teeth and may use their tongues to help them eat.

Do lizards throw up?

When a lizard is sick or has eaten something that doesn't agree with it, it will often throw up. This is sometimes harmful to the lizard because it tends to become dehydrated when this happens.

BLUE TONGUED SKINK ▶

Chapter Five

Lizard Reproduction

How long is gestation?

How big are baby Skinks?

Read on to find the answers to these questions and more.

by Terry Odegaard

How long is gestation?

Some species such as the Shingleback Skink may carry the ***neonates*** for over 100 days while egg-laying species like the Brown Skink carries its eggs for 5 weeks.

How can you tell if a lizard is pregnant?

Females will show signs of pregnancy several different ways. The African Fire Skink will often lay on a heat source when pregnant. The Shingleback Skink may have increased swelling near the stomach area.

How do lizards lay eggs?

As an egg-laying species, the Beaded Dragon will often bury her eggs in a safe, warm, moist place. Lizards lay eggs through their anal plate. Some lizards can lay up to 30 eggs.

How big are baby Skinks?

Baby Skinks vary in size depending on the species. Little Brown Skinks are only 1/2 inch long when born while the Shingleback Skink is about 6-8 inches long when born.

THIS AFRICAN FIRE SKINK IS PREGNANT. SHE WILL HAVE HER BABIES IN A FEW MONTHS. ▶

by Terry Odegaard

How do you tell the difference between male and female lizards?

In some species of lizards, males may be more colorful or larger than the females. In other species, such as Geckos, males may have larger tails than females. Male lizards have hemipenes located in the anal plate which is used for mating.

Do lizards stay as a couple?

Scientists have found that the Shingleback Skink of Australia will stay as a couple for life. Most species of lizards do not display this behavior.

What is the lifespan of a Skink?

According to scientists, the Shingleback Skink can live up to 100 years. On average, most species live 2-10 years.

▲
THIS SHINGLEBACK SKINK CAN LIVE UP TO 100 YEARS.

by Erik D. Stoops

Chapter Six

Self-Defense

What does a Skink do when it feels threatened?

Can a lizard lose its tail?

Read on to find the answers to these questions and more.

What does a Skink do when it feels threatened?

When a Shingleback Skink is scared or feels threatened, it will puff its body with air and stick its tongue out. Other species will hide under logs and rocks to get away from their enemies.

by Terry Odegaard ▲

THIS PRAIRIE SKINK LOST ITS TAIL. THIS DOES NOT HURT THE SKINK AND WILL GROW BACK IN A COUPLE OF MONTHS.

▲ by Terry Christopher

SHINGLEBACK SKINKS USE THEIR TAIL AS A DECOY BECAUSE IT LOOKS LIKE THEIR HEAD.

Can a lizard lose its tail?

Yes. Some species of lizards can lose their tail when they are frightened or need to get away from predators. The tail often grows back in a few months.

Why are lizards' scales so many different colors?

Depending on its geographic location, a lizard's scales may blend in with its surroundings. By doing this, they are able to hide from their predators.

THE AFRICAN FIRE ▶ SKINK IS VERY RED IN COLOR. THE COLOR OF THE SKINK WILL OFTEN HELP IT BLEND IN WITH ITS SUR-ROUNDINGS.

by Terry Odegaard

23

Chapter Seven

Facts about Skinks

Do Skinks have smooth scales?

How do the Skink's bones work?

Read on to find these answers and more.

What is the largest scale on the bottom near the tail of a lizard?

The large scale located between the back legs and near the tail is called an **anal plate**. This is where lizards discharge their wastes and their reproductive organs are located.

by Scottsdale Children's Nature Center

▲

THE SHINGLEBACK SKINK HAS LARGE, HARD, TOUGH SCALES WHICH LOOK LIKE SHINGLES. UNDERNEATH THOSE SCALES IS SOFT SKIN TISSUE.

by Terry Christopher

What is underneath all those scales?

Lizards have several layers of skin under all those scales. These layers of skin help protect the lizard's organs.

Do Skinks have smooth scales?

Yes. Some species of Skinks have smooth scales such as the Prairie Skink. These smooth scales help them burrow in the sand.

25

How do the Skink's bones work?

Lizard bones work like our own bones. They have knees, fingers, ribs and a spinal column. They are often flexible and this helps the lizard move around.

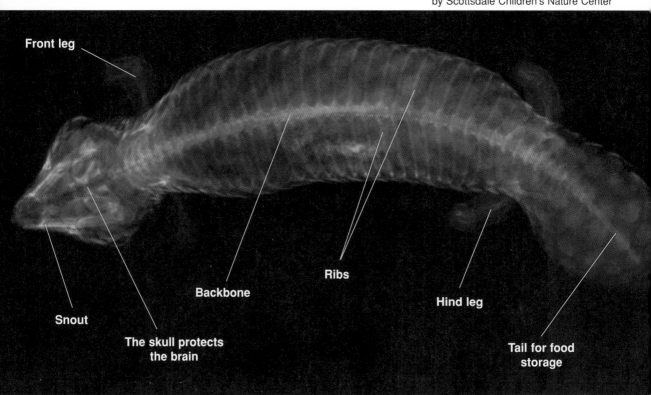

Front leg

Snout

The skull protects the brain

Backbone

Ribs

Hind leg

Tail for food storage

What is the smallest Skink?

The Ground Skink is the smallest species growing to be about 4 inches (10 cm). It is found throughout most of the eastern United States. The young, when born are about 1/2 inch long.

▲ THE LITTLE BROWN SKINK IS A SMALL SPECIES OF LIZARD FOUND IN THE EASTERN UNITED STATES.

What is the largest Skink?

One of the largest Skinks is the Shingleback Skink of Australia. They can reach a length of 2 feet. The babies are almost 8 inches long when born. That's a big baby for a skink.

27

by Terry Christopher

Do Skinks move around a lot?

The Skink family contains some members that are considered the slowest moving of all lizards. Some species may rest on branches and not move all day.

◀ A SLOW SPECIES OF LIZARD IS THE SOLOMON ISLAND SKINK. THEY ARE LIKE THE SLOTHS OF THE LIZARD WORLD.

If I want to be a scientist and study lizards, what will I be?

by Terry Christopher

If you want to study lizards when you grow up, you can become a *herpetologist.* Many herpetologists spend their whole lives trying to protect and conserve different species of lizards.

THE AFRICAN FIRE SKINK IS A GREAT LIZARD ▶ TO STUDY AND DO BOOK REPORTS ON.

What do lizards die from?

Many lizards die from *viruses* and bacteria which they can catch from other lizards. Lizards can catch colds and cough and sneeze like we do. They also die from stress or diseases such as cancer or tumors due to being held in captivity. They can die from *parasites* that crawl on their body and some which live in their body. *Poachers* may often kill lizards for their skin or catch them to sell to people. This is not very fair to the lizards.

by Terry Odegaard

THE FIVE-LINED SKINK IS A POPULAR PET WITH PEOPLE. MOST OF THE TIME, THE LIZARDS DO NOT LIVE VERY LONG BECAUSE THEY ARE NOT KEPT IN THE RIGHT CONDITIONS.

What can I do to protect Skinks?

The best thing to do to protect Skinks is to pick up litter and throw it in a garbage receptacle, and just leave them alone. You should learn more about the Skinks in your area so you can help protect them. It is very rewarding when you do this and it makes you feel good.

◄ THIS LAKE HABITAT IS A HOME FOR MANY SPECIES OF SKINKS. THE BEST THING YOU CAN DO TO HELP LIZARDS IS TO MAKE SURE THEIR HOME IS KEPT FREE FROM POLLUTION.

by Terry Odegaard

Glossary

Anal Plate:
The large scale between the back legs of the lizard.

Chlamydosaurus King II:
A scientific name for frilled lizard.

Cold-Blooded:
Having a body temperature not internally regulated, but approximately that of the environment.

Endangered: Threatened with extinction.

Endemic:
Native to a particular country, nation or region.

External:
Having merely the outward appearance of something.

Fossil:
A remnant impression, or trace of an animal or plant of past geological ages that has been preserved in the earth's crust.

Herpetologist:
One who studies reptiles and amphibians.

Neonate: Newborn.

Paleontologist:
One who studies the science dealing with the life of past geological periods as known from fossil remains.

Parasite:
An organism that lives in or on another organism at whose expense it receives nourishment.

Poacher:
One who kills or takes game and fish illegally.

Quadrupole:
A system composed of two dipoles of equal but oppositely directed moment.

Rhynchocephalian:
A class of reptile.

Scientist:
A scientific investigator.

Unisexual:
All individuals are females that can lay eggs and are fertile without mating.

Virus:
The causative agent of an infectious disease.

Warm-Blooded:
Having a relatively high and constant body temperature relatively independent of the surroundings.

Books and CD-Roms Written by the Author Suggested Reading

Snakes and Other Reptiles of the Southwest

Erik D. Stoops & Annette T. Wright. 1991. Golden West Publishing Company, Phoenix, Arizona. Scientific Field Guide.

Snakes

Erik D. Stoops & Annette T. Wright. 1992. Hardback and Paperback. Sterling Publishing Company, New York. Children's non-fiction, full-color, question and answer format. First Book in Children's Nature Library Series.

Breeding Boas and Pythons

Erik D. Stoops & Annette T. Wright. 1993. TFH Publishing Company, New York. Scientific Care and Breeding Guide.

Sharks

Erik D. Stoops & Sherrie L. Stoops. Illustrated by Jeffrey L. Martin. June, 1994. Hardback and Paperback. Sterling Publishing Company, New York. Children's non-fiction, full-color, question and answer format. Second Book in Children's Nature Library Series.

Dolphins

Erik D. Stoops, Jeffrey L. Martin & Debbie L. Stone. Release date, January, 1995. Hardback and Paperback. Sterling Publishing Company, New York. Children's non-fiction, full-color, question and answer format. Third Book in Children's Nature Library Series.

Whales

Erik D. Stoops, Jeffrey L. Martin & Debbie L. Stone. Release date, March, 1995. Hardback and Paperback. Sterling Publishing Company, New York. Children's non-fiction, full-color, question and answer format. Fourth Book in Children's Nature Library Series.

Scorpions and Other Venomous Insects of the Desert

Erik D. Stoops & Jeffrey L. Martin. Release date, June, 1995. Golden West Publishing Company, Phoenix, Arizona. A user-friendly guide.

Alligators and Crocodiles

Erik D. Stoops & Debbie L. Stone. Release date, October, 1994. Sterling Publishing Company, New York. Children's non-fiction, full-color, question and answer format. Fifth Book in Children's Nature Library Series.

Wolves

Erik D. Stoops & Dagmar Fertl. Release date, December, 1996. Sterling Publishing Company, New York. Children's non-fiction, full-color, question and answer format. Sixth Book in Children's Nature Library Series.

Internet Sites:

Zoo Net:
http://www.mindspring.com/~zoonet

Herp Link:
http://home.ptd.net/~herplink/index.html

Erik Stoops:
http://www.primenet.com/~dink

Look for the Adventures of Dink the Skink Children's book series and animated CD Rom Stories coming out in 1997.

INDEX

Beaded Dragon, 20

Birth, 7, 20

Bones, 26

Colors, of bodies, 21, 23

Death, 29

Dinosaurs, 6

Ears, 6, 12

Eating Habits, 7, 14-17

Eggs, 19-20

Enemies, 23

Environment, 7-9, 29

Eyelids, 4, 6

Eyes, 13

Gestation, 19

Glossary, 30

Illness, 16-17, 29

Interesting Facts, 23-29

Jacobson's Organ, 13

Lifespan, 21

Limbs, 6, 26

Mating, 18-21

Protection of, 29

Scales, 23-25

Self-defense, 12, 22-23

Senses, 10-13

Sight, 13, 17

Size, 7, 20, 27

Skin, 13, 25

Snout, 13, 26

Species, 6-7, 9

African Fire Skink,
6, 12, 20, 23, 28

Blue-Tongued Skink,
5, 7, 15-17

Five-Lined Skink, 29

Ground Skink, 27

Little Brown Skink,
16, 19-20, 27

Prairie Skink, 16, 23, 25

Sand Skink, 13

Shingleback Skink, 6-7,
12-13, 16, 19-21, 23, 25-27

Solomon Island Skink,
11, 25, 28

Spiny-Tailed Skink, 7

Tail, 6-7, 21, 23, 26

Teeth, 17

Tongue, 7, 17

WE WOULD LIKE TO THANK THE FOLLOWING PEOPLE FOR THEIR ENCOURAGEMENT AND PARTICIPATION:
NATIONAL ZOOLOGICAL PARK, OFFICE OF PUBLIC AFFAIRS, SUSAN BIGGS, SMITHSONIAN INSTITUTION,
TERRY CHRISTOPHER, TERRY ODEGAARD, CINCINNATI ZOO AND BOTANICAL GARDENS, ST. LOUIS ZOO,
BILL LUBACK'S REPTILES, INC., AMANDA JAKSHA, JESSIE COHEN, PAT TURCOTT, RODNEY FREEMAN,
DIANE E. FREEMAN, STEVEN CASTANEDA, CLYDE PEELINGS OF REPTILELAND, MICKEY OLSEN OF WILDLIFE
WORLD ZOO, SCOTTSDALE CHILDREN'S NATURE CENTER, DR. JEAN ARNOLD, ARIZONA GAME AND
FISH DEPARTMENT, ERIN DEAN OF THE UNITED STATES FISH AND WILDLIFE SERVICE,
BOB FAULKNER, DAVE PFEIFFER OF EDUCATION ON WHEELS FOR MAKING THIS PROJECT A REALITY,
DR. MARTY FELDMAN, SHERRIE STOOPS, ALESHA STOOPS, VICTORIA AND JESSICA EMERY.